A Pictorial Guide To

The Malvern Hills

An illustrated study and exploration
of the Malvern Hills

Book One: North Malvern, West Malvern and
Malvern Link

by Carl Flint FRSA

Published by Malvern Walks
Aldine Print Limited,
Barnards Green Road,
Malvern
WR14 3NB

First published in Great Britain 2010

ISBN 978-0-9566295-0-0

2 4 6 8 10 9 7 5 3

Published by Malvern Walks and printed in Great Britain by Orchard Press (Cheltenham Ltd), Northway Trading Estate, Tewkesbury GL20 8JH

This book is dedicated to
Fiona Mackay who inspired
me to write

Author's Note

The Wainwright series of pictorial guides made a huge impression on me as a youngster. My parents took to walking quite late on in life and started buying 'Wainwrights', when I was in my teens. When my parents went on their walks, my sister Sharron and I would be shipped off to the grandparents and later we would hear on their return, the tales of 'mud up to our knees', gargantuan breakfasts served in a wonderful countryside pub and then a few weeks later suffer the multitude of slides showed inevitably after dinner on a Saturday.

We would listen to the tales of trudging along Offas Dyke in the rain or trying to make out the craggy features of Scarfell in the mist. I distinctly have the memory that the English weather attempted to reduce everything to the lowest common denominator of damp and cold, seemingly even in July. However, these muddy stories sowed the seeds of the walking gene which was to remain with me for the rest of my life.

You do not have to be a backpacker type to enjoy the Malverns. They are, in comparison to the North Yorkshire Moors, The Derbyshire Peak District and the Lake District significantly smaller in area but arguably equally rich in the cultural diversity and heritage of this designated area of Outstanding Natural Beauty.

Hopefully there will be time before an excursion into the 'Hills', to digest the contents of this book and decide which walk to enjoy first.

I hope when you read through this Pictorial Guide in the comfort of your own home, the wet, the mud and the simple joy of a fantastic view across miles of English countryside are all there to fill up your senses. Enjoy.

To conclude, The Malvern Hills is the book never written by Wainwright. It is written in his style as homage to him and his love of the countryside. His fanatical dedication over a great many years to document the beautiful English countryside is without parallel. This book will grow as later editions are published, hopefully enhanced by contributions from like-minded people. All submissions will be acknowledged on the website www.malvernwalks.co.uk and in the following reprint. So thank you in advance! The Malverns are a large part of my life. I hope you get as much pleasure as I do from your experiences on The Malvern Hills.

Maubon hills, or as some term them, the English Alps – a Ridge of hills dividing Worcestershire and Herifordshire, and was formerly esteemed the divideing England and Wales, Herriford, Shropshire, etc, were Weltch Countys. They are at least 2 or 3 miles up and are in a Pirramidy fashion on the top.

The Malvern Hills are designated as an Area of Outstanding Natural Beauty (AONB). The Hills will only retain this status if all of us who visit the area are aware of the impact we personally make upon the landscape, whether walking, jogging or mountain biking. In enjoying the natural beauty of the Hills and the stunning views, do something positive. Can I suggest a piece of litter is picked up per walk, as every little helps!

Acknowledgements

My family took an active interest in helping me accumulate the material I needed for this book and on occasions 'groaned' at the prospect of trekking out to a distant corner of the Hills to confirm a statement. Many friends have also helped with proof-reading and verifying the details in the walks. In particular, Dr. Cyril Edwards, Justine Sissons and Jerry Greer were merciless with their red pens at every missed comma and semi-colon. Su Savage, freelance designer, took the raw ingredients of my text and pictures and has created an attractive, appealing design and easy to follow layout. I hope you will enjoy reading the 'Pictorial Guide' and find it a useful and trustworthy companion in your enjoyment of The Malvern Hills.

New roads are built, footpaths 'disappear', boundaries change and hostelries can be 'under new management', all of which ensures this book is out of date before it is published. Any contributions and corrections forwarded to the website www.malvernwalks.co.uk will be published in the next edition along with the name of the contributor. Thank you in advance!

Contents

Book One

North Malvern, West Malvern and Malvern Link

Chapter

1	Introduction	10
2	North Malvern to West Malvern	25
	Walk 1 The Clock Tower, North Malvern to West Malvern via Table Hill and End Hill, circular walk	33
3	Malvern Link to North Malvern returning via Great Malvern	68
	Walk 2 Malvern Link to North Hill via Cowleigh. Returning by St Ann's Well and Great Malvern	77
4	Hostelries	143
	Bibliography	150
	Contributors	152
	Web Addresses	153
	Index	155

Introduction

The 'Pictorial Guide to the Malvern Hills' has been written for the rambler, jogger, mountain biker and tourist to enjoy and experience the breathtaking splendour of The Malvern Hills and the surrounding area.

There are fifteen walks to enjoy in this series of four publications. Each book illustrates an area of the Malverns. The books and walks are set out in a clockwise rotation around the Hills, starting with the northern hills first. Each walk is individual and draws upon the characteristics of the area, whether it is local history, the beauty of the views, the unique springs and wells, or the sheer pleasure of walking through some of the most outstanding and diverse countryside England has to offer.

The Malverns are claimed to be 200 to 250 million years old. Therefore, older than the Alps, Andes or the Himalayas. The rocks that make up the Malverns are a form of granite from the Pre-Cambrian age, and are said to be at least 600 million years old. So when walking on the Malverns, you are really experiencing the heritage of planet earth.

With regard to the conservation of the Malvern Hills, there is a publicly funded body known as the Conservators (not Conservatives!), whose reason for existence is to manage and protect the 3,000 acres of the Malvern Hills and Commons. The Malvern Hills Conservators are the second oldest conservation body in Britain, and were set up by Parliament in 1884, as an elected body to manage and protect the heritage of the Hills for future generations. They also manage most of the car parks on the Hills and Commons, from which the revenue contributes towards the conservation of the Hills.

For further information about the Conservators log on to their website at: -
www.malvernhills.org.uk

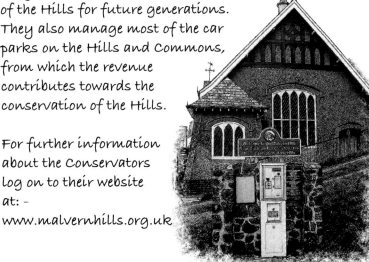

Malverns finest days were as a spa town during the Victorian era, and to this day the spring water continues to be sold throughout the world.

Great Malvern from the Priory Bell Tower

It is allegedly the only bottled water Her Royal Highness, Queen Elizabeth will drink. Not only is the Malvern area famous for its spring water, it is well known for the music it inspired Elgar to compose, the misty mountains of Tolkien, the gas lamp at the entrance to Narnia, the Morgan sports car, the invention of radar and right up to date, the invention of the Liquid Crystal Display.

Getting There

The Malvern Hills are easily approached from the Midlands, Wales and Southwest England, principally by the M5, to the east and the M50, to the southwest. Exiting Junction 7 of the M5 via the Worcester A422 ring or 'Link Road' as it is locally known will take the average motorist 25 minutes to reach the Hills from the motorway, unless you are unlucky enough to catch a car boot sale on a Sunday morning at the Tewkesbury turn-off, or delayed by extra traffic heading for an event at the Three Counties Showground.

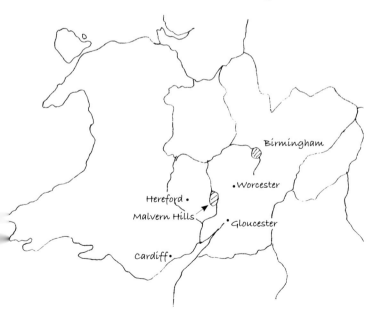

Visiting the Malverns whilst taking in a show at the Three Counties appeals to a large number of people, especially in the spring and summer months. The most famous of these events are the Spring and Autumn Garden Shows, which are featured on all respectable television gardening programmes.

From Central Wales, the A4103 Hereford to Worcester Road, is somewhat tortuous especially at peak times owing to the single carriageway for the majority of its length. For the north section of the hills (Walks 1 and 2), turn off at Storridge on the B4219. Speed cameras in Leigh Sinton and Fromes Hill serve to catch the unwary.

The M50, provides three different options to visit the area. If travelling from the west, the Junction 2 exit onto the A417 provides a route via the charming market town of Ledbury, and then onto the A449 which winds its way through delightful countryside to the British Camp (Book 3) and onto Great Malvern.

For those travelling to the area from the South,
Junction 1 of the M50, via the A38 and the
A4104, through the lively town
of Upton upon Severn will
take 20 minutes to reach
Little Malvern Priory
(Walk 7) on a good day,
except during the popular
Upton International
Jazz Festival week
in June each
year.

A different route, leading to the southern most
hills from Junction 2 on the M50, is to turn
onto the A417, heading for Gloucester. The road
returns over the motorway and after a short
distance, follow the signpost for Redmarley
D'Abitot.

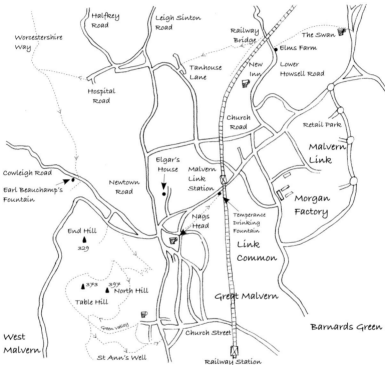

Turn left, and head in the direction of the
signposted 'The Malverns', on the B4208. Then
turn left again onto the A438, signposted Eastnor
and Ledbury; this leads to the southern end of the
Hills at Hollybush (Walks 9 and 10).

Great Malvern
Railway Station

For the
environmentally
conscious, Malvern Link,
Great Malvern and Colwall
are accessible by train from Birmingham, London
Paddington and Hereford. In general there are trains
once every two hours to London Paddington, with a
journey time of 2 hours 40 minutes and two trains
an hour to Birmingham with a journey time of 58
minutes or the slower train of 1 hour 20 minutes.

Malvern Link
Railway Station

Coach travel to the Malverns is less frequent than trains. There are two coaches each way every day to London Victoria with a journey time of approximately five hours.

For those interested in linking up with national walks, the 'Worcestershire Way' follows the north–south alignment of the Hills and has its own chapter in Book 4.

Getting around the Malverns with the Malvern Hills Hopper Bus.

Please note that shortly before publication, Malvernian Tours in Newtown Road, sadly went into liquidation. The following has been retained with the hope that another provider will take on the route and ensure this magical tour around the Malverns continues.

My first experience of this wonderful inexpensive local bus was one Sunday morning. The early start proved a little difficult to achieve with three children to get ready and two friends up for the weekend, who had very generously shared a large container of Knights cider (see Walk 2) the previous evening.

Whilst many may think of a 'Hopper Bus' as a utilitarian vehicle, the Malvern Hopper is by definition different. My first trip on the Hopper described here, was in a handsome old-fashioned 1950's coach with gleaming paintwork. The interior was laid out with wooden tables nestling between upholstered seats, allowing, if one so wished, a quick round of gin rummy whilst en route. Subsequent trips more recently have proved less romantic, with the use of a modern coach complete with seat belts.

This very special tourist coach service only operates on Saturday, Sunday and Bank Holiday Mondays from Easter until the end of October. It provides an ideal opportunity to explore the Hills and further afield as far as the picturesque towns of Ledbury and Upton upon Severn. The circular route has 27 drop-off and pick-up points, where one is free to stop, explore and get back on the bus over the course of a day, as many times as is wished.

The starting point for the Hopper is Malvernian Tours in Newtown Road, Malvern Link Top, map reference SO 7740 4769 (for further details see walk 2). The first bus heads down from Newtown Road to Richmond Road in Malvern Link at 08.45. The second bus, at 10.45. A pause for lunch, then at 13.15, followed by 15.15 and the last bus 17.15.

Each journey takes 1³/₄ hours, and stops at the principal locations of Malvern Link, Barnards Green, Great Malvern Railway Station, Link Top, West Malvern, the Wyche Cutting, British Camp, Malvern Wells, the Three Counties Showground, Hanley Swan, Upton upon Severn, Welland, Castlemorton Common, Hollybush, Eastnor Castle and Ledbury, before heading back via British Camp to Malvern Link Top. The all-day fare for an adult is under £3, and a family ticket a very modest £5. Travelling with a bicycle is not a problem and the bus will also carry wheelchairs. For more up-to-date information log on to: - www.malvernhillsaonb.org.uk

References to other supporting materials to make a visit more enjoyable.

The Ordnance Survey Landranger series 150 maps, have a scale of 1:50,000, and give a good overview of the area. Better still, The Ordnance Survey Explorer Map 190, Malvern Hills & Bredon Hills, gives the level of detail necessary to discover the nooks and crannies of this area of outstanding natural beauty. The scale is 1:25,000, which equates to 4cm to 1km (2¹/₂ inches to 1 mile in old currency). The Bredon Hills are to the East of the Malverns, beyond Pershore and the River Avon.

Of particular interest is the series of three 1:10,000 scale maps of the Malvern Hills; this equates to 10 cm to 1 km or 6.3 inches to 1 mile. Map 1 is North Malvern to The Wyche. Map 2, The Wyche to British Camp, and Map 3, British Camp to Chase End. There is also the Harvey Map of the Malvern Hills, with the same detailed scale of 1:10,000. All of these specialist interest maps provide the level of detail to really experience the intricacies of the Hills.

Map and Grid References used in this book

Note, the use of eight-digit 'map and grid' references are interchangeable. For example the railway bridge by the Link Station, map reference SO 7820 4741, could also be described as a grid reference.

Map Symbols

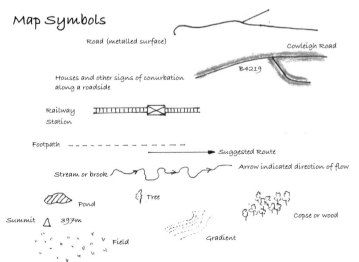

Road (metalled surface)

Cowleigh Road

B4219

Houses and other signs of conurbation along a roadside

Railway Station

Footpath

Suggested Route

Stream or brook

Arrow indicated direction of flow

Pond

Tree

Copse or wood

Summit   397m

Field

Gradient

Two books stand out as an excellent source of local knowledge, Brian Smith's 'A History of Malvern', and 'Aquae Malvernensis', by Cora Weaver and Bruce Osborne. The latter book describes in detail the springs and spouts around the Malvern Hills. A bibliography of other supporting material, along with an index, is located at the end of this guide.

Beacon Books (Telephone 01684 564939), is a large independent bookshop at Number 25 Worcester Road in Great Malvern. The Malvern Bookshop (formerly the site of the R. Lechmere's bookshop, whose family can be traced back to the Norman Conquest and has played an important part in the history of Worcestershire), provides a good selection of second-hand books, Telephone 01684 575915. It is located in the attractive Priory Steps, just off Belle Vue Island alongside the Lyttelton House Gallery and the Great Malvern Delicatessen.

Priory
Steps

The Tourist Information Centre, 21 Church Street, WR14 2AA, opposite the Belle Vue Island provides as expected, a wealth of local information, telephone 01684 892872.

Further afield, 'The Map Shop' in Upton upon Severn is renowned county-wide for providing a substantial range of maps and books of local and international interest. Contact details for the Map Shop are: 15 High Street, Upton upon Severn, WR8 0HJ, Telephone 0800 0854080. They are open Monday to Saturday 9.00-5.30 pm.

How this book is organised

After the introduction, the two walks follow a north-south clockwise rotation of the Malvern Hills. Subsequent books continue this circular mapping of the Hills. Each walk is written in a similar format for consistency. The local history and places of interest in the vicinity of the walk are described. This is followed by a summary, the distance, predicted time to complete, availability of refreshments, location of wells, springs and spouts, places of interest and the interconnection to other walks.

Many of the drawings printed throughout the book are either drawn by myself or are digitally generated using Akvis software.

This specialist software package converts photographs into a black and white line drawing style. I trust that the combination of these images and commentary will begin to recreate on paper the magic of the Malverns.

orth Malvern to West Malvern

History

The development of North
Malvern began chiefly
during the late eighteenth
century with the
completion of the road
around North
Hill, joining West
Malvern with Link Top
and Great Malvern.
A number of significant
infrastructure projects such as the Clock Tower,
reservoir and school were instigated
and financed by Charles
Morris (1799-1856),
who was the
grandson of
James Morris,
Deputy
Lieutenant of
Surrey and
High Sheriff.

The numerous paths that can be seen carved into North Hill, and the smaller End Hill, tell their own history.

One of the paths was known as the 'Pyx Path' and used by the priests from Worcester, when they brought sacrament to the hermits of Malvern in St. Werstan's and St. Aldwyn's days. Another story suggests that the path was named the Pixie Path by which the 'Pharisees' (pixies or fairies) entered their settlement on North Hill. It is said that the building of the clock tower and reservoirs in the 1880's, drove them away forever! A rather less interesting definition for the Pyx Path is Pig Path. It is suggested that these paths were formed over time by farmers driving their pigs across the hills!

The community of West Malvern circumnavigates the northwest area of the Hills, with its homes clinging to the steep slopes facing the undulating Worcestershire– Herefordshire countryside, and beyond into Wales. Every year in July this small neighbourhood opens its doors, or more accurately the playing field to circa 5,000 people enjoying the live music, local arts and crafts of the 'West Fest'. The playing field is located to the west of the Old Hollow Road, map reference SO 7685 4698. The roads in the whole area become severely congested during the festival, therefore it is advisable to park a fair distance away and walk in. It will be quicker and less fraught!

On a more sombre note, Peter Mark Roget of 'Roget's Thesaurus' fame is buried in West Malvern in the cemetery of St. James's Church. He died in 1869, at the ripe old age of 90, whilst on holiday in West Malvern.

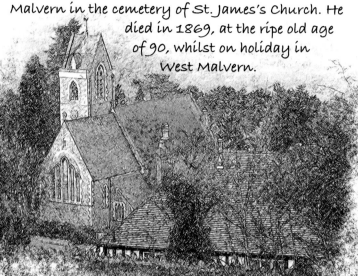

He is widely known for his publication in 1852, 'The Thesaurus of English Words and Phrases'. He also helped found the School of Medicine at the University of Manchester and invented the logarithmic slide rule (which many of us learnt to use before the invention of the calculator).

More recently, in 1998, the Malvern Hills Brewery established itself on the West Malvern Road, a short distance up from the Clock Tower in North Malvern.

The North Malvern Quarries

The scars caused by quarrying on the North Hill are still very much evident today.

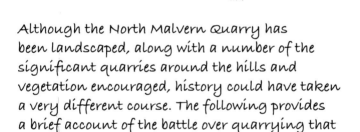

Although the North Malvern Quarry has been landscaped, along with a number of the significant quarries around the hills and vegetation encouraged, history could have taken a very different course. The following provides a brief account of the battle over quarrying that raged for 140 years.

The pre-Cambrian stone which makes up most of the Malverns is very difficult to cut owing to its hardness and does not readily fracture into slabs. Therefore with the advent of the motor car, the irregular lumps of rock were in great demand as hardcore and later mixed with tar to form the macadam surface used in making roads everywhere.

With the passing of the first Malvern Hills Act in 1884, rights to quarry stone on a small scale were given to landowners by the Conservators, as the main issues of the act were concerned with encroachment. In 1886,  the Conservators were able to close some quarries but the Gardiner, Summer and Price quarries continued with production. By 1887, complaints from locals were flooding in deploring the disfigurement of North and End Hills.

By 1907, the Conservators were petitioned by the local people because of concern over the substantial volume of stone being cut and transported from the Hills. The resulting wear and tear on the roads and infrastructure was significant, causing a groundswell of lobbying against the quarry companies. The Conservators investigated how they might legally modify the previous Act to stop the quarrying and in turn compensate the landowners and companies, who were mining the heart out of the Malvern Hills.

In 1909, the Conservators managed to present an amended Act to Parliament but the House of Lords was not convinced that the Conservators could sufficiently compensate the landowners, and the bill was stripped of all the clauses which had been passionately fought over. It was eventually passed with amendments to increase the rating powers of the Conservators to increase the precept and a slight modification to the constitution. The Conservators did not have the funds or reserves to compensate the landowners and in turn had expended virtually all of their income on legal costs, which in 1909 amounted to £3,000.

As the First World War indulged in its slaughter of millions across the mud of Flanders, Malvern was destined to become little more than a stone-quarrying town. The final legacy of the water cure had disappeared some thirty years earlier, and it seemed Malvern was doomed to self-destruction through quarrying of its family heirloom. However, the scars caused by the quarries were reaching such pervading proportions that a groundswell of revolt and lobbying reached a select committee in the House of Lords in 1924, and fortunately for those of us who enjoy the amazing splendour of the Hills, the third Malvern Hills Act was passed and the quarrying ceased forever.

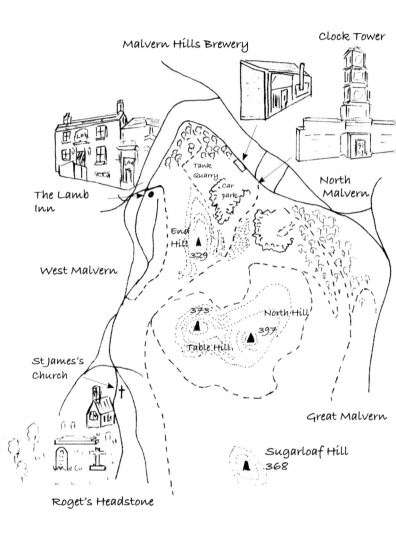

Clock Tower

Malvern Hills Brewery

The Lamb Inn

North Malvern

Tank Quarry

car park

West Malvern

End Hill
329

373

North Hill
397

Table Hill

St James's Church

Great Malvern

Sugarloaf Hill
368

Roget's Headstone

Walk 1.

he Clock Tower, North Malvern to West
Malvern via Table Hill and End Hill,
circular walk

Summary
This short walk starts from either the North Hill
Quarry or the Tank Quarry car parks on the
North Malvern Road, map reference SO 7705
4700. Following the climb past the Clock Tower
there is a steep path up to Table Hill, and therefore
this walk is not suitable for pushing buggies or
for very young children. There are far-reaching
views across Herefordshire to the west, Shropshire
to the far north-west with the Severn Valley and
Worcestershire to the east. The return journey is
via the Westminster Spout and West Malvern.

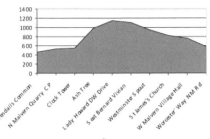

Distance, time and altitude
This walk is just 2.3 miles. Allow 1 hour 45 minutes without rest, refreshment breaks or stops. North Hill 397 metres, (1303 feet), Table Hill 372 metres, End Hill 329 metres

Refreshments
The Lamb Inn

Wells, Springs and Spouts

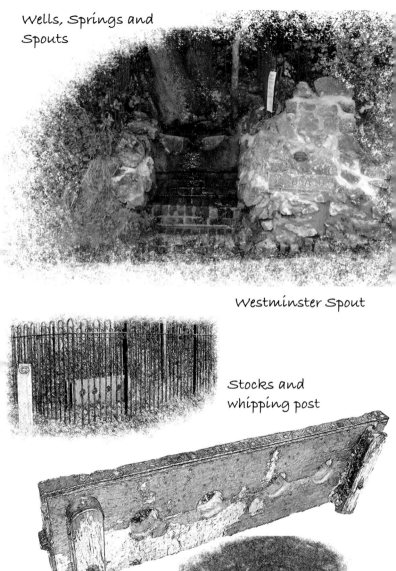

Westminster Spout

Stocks and whipping post

Danzell Spring

Places and points of interest

The Clock Tower

Lady Howard De Walden Drive

Malvern
Hills
Brewery

Roget's headstone in the cemetery of St. James's Church, West Malvern

The former St James's School and stately home

Connections to other walks
Walk 2 Malvern Link to North Malvern via
Cowleigh. Returning via St Ann's Well and
Great Malvern.
Walk 14 All the Hills End to End.

The walk starts either from the North Hill Quarry
car park or the Tank Quarry car park, which are
located on either side of the Clock Tower. Please
note that it is nigh impossible to park on the West
Malvern Road as it circumnavigates the Hills. It
is very narrow and what parking spaces there are,
are taken by the locals; so if possible park your
charabanc, in one of the Conservators car parks as
described here.

From the North Hill Quarry car park.
From Great Malvern town centre, head north in the
direction of Worcester along the Worcester Road;
after approximately
half a mile take the
first turning on the
left into the North
Malvern Road.
It is signposted
West Malvern and
Bromyard. Shortly
after the turning
on the left, there is a
local site of interest, the old
stocks and whipping post.

They are situated behind wrought iron railings at the junction of Lodge Drive and the North Malvern Road.

Opposite the Holy Trinity Church. Next to the railings is a small MHC (Malvern Hills Conservators) plaque on a wooden post indicating the site of Kendalls Common, map reference SO 7746 4684.

The small cast-iron pillar next to the footpath is all that remains of a drinking fountain.

Continue for a third of a mile and the North Hill car park will be on the left. Map reference SO 7705 4700.

If parked in the North Hill Quarry, then there is an option to pick up walk 1. However, to start this walk head down to the car park exit and back onto the North Malvern Road; turn left heading uphill to the refurbished Clock Tower

(Map Reference SO 7695 4707), comes into view.

Now skip the next three paragraphs and continue reading from 'The North Malvern Clock Tower

From the Tank Quarry car park.
For those who have parked in the Tank Quarry car park; this has undergone resurfacing and so provides modern spacious parking. Adjacent is a lush, grassy area for picnics. It is a gated car park, opened and closed by a local resident. Times are displayed at the entrance. There is no direct access to the Hills from the car park. There are signs displaying 'access permitted for the Malvern Hills Outdoor Centre, no public access'.

The Geological Trail located around the north end of the car park provides interesting examples and descriptions of the rocks

which
make up the
Malvern Hills. The
covered information signboard also
provides a good deal of local information.

Apparently, the Tank Quarry was featured in an old (1968), episode of Doctor Who! Head down the metalled roadway back to the North Malvern Road, turn right towards the Clock Tower.

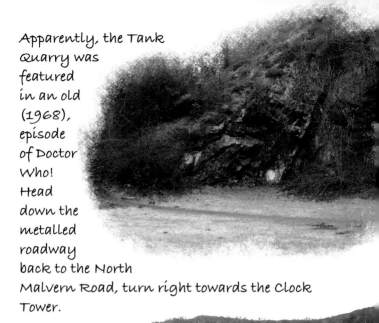

The North Malvern Clock Tower

This was built in 1843, and paid for by Charles Morris (1799-1856). The Clock Tower was built for the benefit of the local inhabitants. Originally the circular inscription dated 1901, was the location for the clock face.

In 1901, the Urban District Council took on the repairs and extended the height of the tower with the permission of the owner Mr C W Dyson Perrins (of Lee and Perrins Worcestershire Sauce fame).

After 106 years, the Clock Tower was subject to a timely refurbishment during 2007, this time with money made available through the National Heritage Lottery Fund. The Clock Tower was in quite a poor state, and in danger of being irrevocably damaged by the growth of nearby trees. These were cut down, the brickwork re-pointed, the clock repaired and a new set of attractive iron gates now proudly protect the interior.

Charles Morris was a major benefactor for North Malvern. He provided the finance to install large tanks dug into the hillside to create a reservoir of clean running water for the people of North Malvern. He was the grandson of James Morris, Deputy Lieutenant of Surrey and High Sheriff. Charles had a brother, James (d.1883), who was Governor of the Bank of England.

Opposite the clock tower, is the former Morris School for Girls and Infants, which has recently been converted to flats.

Its original development was financially supported by Charles Morris and was opened in 1838. From 1942 to 1991, it continued as the North Malvern Infants School. Heading down the road is the old North Malvern School for Boys. Opposite, cut into the grassy bank, is a flight of steps, which in spring is set amongst a carpet of snowdrops; this leads up into the North Hill Quarry car park.

After viewing the unusual Clock Tower and the recently refurbished inscription,

> 'The inhabitants of North Malvern place this stone here to record that these tanks were erected at the sole expense of Charles Morris Jn Esq. of Portman Sq London in 1835 and 1836. The young and aged, poor pray that the blessing of God be beneficially poured on him who has here poured abundant blessing upon you'.

Take the steps immediately to the right of the Tower, they lead up to the location of the former spout, and above the spout archway is an inscription, warning that 'any person once found wilfully damaging this reservoir will be prosecuted according to law'. This has replaced a former inscription, which read, 'any persons found damaging the reservoir will be called to task!'

The route climbs steeply up a twisting path of
steps, laid down in the last century towards
a number of fir trees; this leads to a choice of
routes. In front is an impressive central staircase
enclosed by a canopy of fir trees heading up to a
level grassy plateau (above the reservoir tanks)
and ideal for picnics. However, take the more
rugged steep flight of steps to the left, which
circumnavigates the fir trees. The path has the
occasional railing for protection and support.

There is a fine outlook over the Clock Tower and North Malvern and also over the picnic area described previously.

The bracken and gorse-edged path climbs steeply in the nape of the valley with underfoot a lot of loose rock, towards the open expanse of the Hills, and ahead in the distance, the remains of an ash tree.

Thus far, just 0.2 of a mile has been covered since leaving the Clock Tower, although it seems further because of the climb.

The remains of the ash tree act as the focal point to a number of paths,

map reference SO 7680 4668. The lateral path crossing from right to left heads up to the clearly chiselled path circumnavigating End Hill and North Hill, called the Lady Howard De Walden Drive.

Our walk for today heads straight uphill avoiding the steep rock face of the Tank Quarry to the left. Ensure the narrow, but clearly defined path, with bramble bushes either side is taken up onto the Drive along the base of the valley. Further to the left is North Hill, straight ahead is Table Hill, and to the right is End Hill. Continuing the ascent, the path now joins the broad Lady Howard De Walden Drive and a much needed wooden bench. Map reference SO 7680 4649.

Take a rest following this first half hour's steep climb and enjoy the vista towards Malvern Link and Worcester. Surprisingly when trying to pick out the River Severn, given its size it can only be seen with binoculars or when in flood.

To note; the broad drive follows the contours of the hills and after approximately half a mile heading in a south easterly direction, it intersects with Walk 2.

Cross over the drive and continue uphill on the broad grassy slope of Table Hill. On reaching the highest point of this path, there is the saddle between the two hills, either head north to End Hill (329m), which is to the right, or to the left (south), to the slightly higher North Hill (397m).

After enjoying the achievement of reaching the gentle summits of either or both hills, take time to study the spectacle of the panoramas across Herefordshire to the west, Shropshire to the far north-west and Worcestershire to the east. Head downhill in a westerly direction, keeping Green Valley to the left. Traverse the Herefordshire side of Table Hill, keeping to the path cut into the grassy hillside. On reaching a relatively flat area where a number of paths intersect, crossing the hills north–south and east-west, aim for the wrought iron post.

A little further ahead is a small wooden bench overlooking the rolling Herefordshire countryside. Continue past this bench and after that there is a wide path bearing in a northerly direction and another seat: this has the plaque; to Bernard Vivian, who died in 1980, with treasured memories. Map reference SO 7661 4620.

West Malvern is now visible with the Tower of
St James's church and the impressive Victorian
stately home which was until recently St James's
School.

The wide
descending track
skirts Table
Hill and loses
height, meeting
a rising stony
path running
along the edge of
the fields. This
path forms part of
the latter stages
of the gruelling
Beacon Race
Route (see Walk 5).

Turning left, head downhill; there is a large
wooden five-bar gate set into the stone wall and
to the side, low-down, just discernible, is a sign
for West Malvern
carved in
stone.

Just a
few
paces
further downhill there is a small plaque depicting
Joyner's Meadow, next to the wooden kissing gate
and footpath sign.

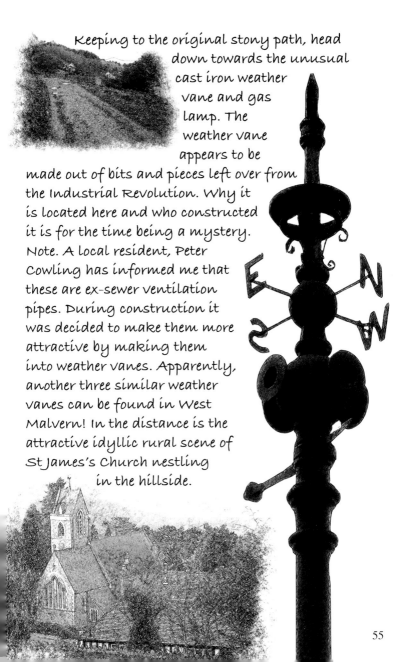

Keeping to the original stony path, head down towards the unusual cast iron weather vane and gas lamp. The weather vane appears to be made out of bits and pieces left over from the Industrial Revolution. Why it is located here and who constructed it is for the time being a mystery. Note. A local resident, Peter Cowling has informed me that these are ex-sewer ventilation pipes. During construction it was decided to make them more attractive by making them into weather vanes. Apparently, another three similar weather vanes can be found in West Malvern! In the distance is the attractive idyllic rural scene of St James's Church nestling in the hillside.

A little further along the path is the Westminster Spout, map reference SO 7647 4617.

This small spring was recently refurbished in 2007, by English Heritage with Lottery funding. Behind

the spring is a set of manhole covers enclosed within an iron railing fence. These are the various reservoir cisterns (tanks), which supply local residents and the former St James's School; hence the flow rate is little more than a trickle. Opposite the spring is a small seat at the edge of the meadow, providing a picturesque scene of West Malvern.

Thus far the distance from the Clock Tower is 0.7 miles.

Now head down the metalled single track towards the buildings of the accommodation and teaching blocks of the former St James's school and past the dwelling named 'Bank House'. Westminster Bank descends very steeply to the West Malvern Road.

Turning left onto the West Malvern Road, a short distance further on, St James's Church can be found. Map reference SO 7636 4611. Enter the churchyard over the cattle grid and continue past the church. To the left, just past the side entrance to the church, and parallel to the road, is a small spring.

Although there are at least six clay pipes at the back of the structure, it is dry.

Continue a few steps towards the war memorial, and facing towards the graveyard, Peter Roget and his daughter Catherine's large horizontal headstone lies just 10 or so paces into this pretty graveyard, fairly close to the hedge on the left-hand side. Dr. Peter Roget was famous for writing the 'Thesaurus of English Words and Phrases', published in 1852. He died at the age of 90 during one of his regular holidays to Malvern.

Return to the West Malvern Road, and the impressive stately home comes into view, along with the 283 acre site. This was until recently St James's school. It was also the former residence of the De Walden family from 1891 to 1900. To this day, the swimming pool is supplied by fresh Malvern spring water from the Westminster Spout. Head back along the West Malvern Road, go past the junction with Westminster Bank and continue along the pavement. Carry on past the Mathon turning to the left. Head down the West Malvern Road; immediately before reaching a post-box set into the wall on the right, there is a narrow entrance to a bridleway heading uphill. If 'Harmony House' (providing bed and breakfast, phone number 01684 891650) at Number 184 West Malvern Road is reached on the opposite side of the road, then the bridleway has been missed.

This bridleway
can be accessed,
rather than the
road, for a more
interesting
look at the back
gardens, to the
rear of houses
on the West
Malvern Road.
Many of the
gardens have
gates leading
into the hills.
After passing
through a metal
gate, the path
is quite steep
in places and
rocky underfoot.
Keeping to the
bridleway as it
skirts the backs
of gardens, a
charming
tree house
in the
style of a
1930's council
workman's caravan delights the onlooker.

A little further along the path is a concrete plinth to the underground chamber of the Danzell Spring. This source of fresh water was used freely by the locals up to 1896. The total distance of this short excursion can be no more than approximately 400 metres. The path exits through a gate signposted with

'The Worcestershire Way', onto the Lamb Bank Road. This leads down past cottages to The Lamb public house.

This is a popular, well known local hostelry serving excellent beer and good food. Opposite, on the West Malvern Road, is the bus stop for the very irregular bus service between Great Malvern and Ledbury, route number 675.

Alternatively, staying with the road, the West Malvern Social Club and Village Hall are on the right, map reference SO 7645 4666. Continue past the Malvern Hills Outdoor Centre turning on the left, and further on to the

Lamb Bank and Lamb Pub. Continue downhill. It would appear that for the construction companies that built these houses during the last two centuries, they had to contend with conditions similar to Switzerland.

The Worcestershire Way (see Book 4), descends from this section of the walk by Number 72 West Malvern Road (map reference SO 7661 4729), and heads down a very steep flight of steps to the Old Hollow Road.

The steps are difficult to find as they are tucked in between two houses.

Continue walking downhill, around the sweeping right-hand bend past the West Malvern Road sign; on the right at the apex of the bend, the footpath leads into the woods heading up to End Hill. As the road straightens out, on the right is a short terrace of houses rather strangely named Hockilwah Villas. The name might suggest a German connection; however for the time being the origin of the name of this small terrace remains a mystery!

The Malvern Hills Brewery is located besides the last house of the terrace, Number 15

West Malvern Road, in a very small unattractive
building, which apparently used to be a
gunpowder store. Peering in through the windows
will reveal that the
building is

packed with
fermentation equipment.
The brewery was founded in 1998 by Julian
Hawthornwaite, who previously brewed beers as a
hobby.

He produces 40 barrels of bitter every week. The
beers are named after local celebrities and icons,
such as Red Earl, Black Pear, Dr Gulley's Winter
Ale and Moel Bryn. They are sold as far and
wide as Cumbria! For more information, visit
the website at www.malvernhillsbrewery.co.uk or
Telephone 01684 577336.

Opposite the brewery, a sculptured 'knight' standing guard has been created during the construction of an external wall to a building. Continuing downhill and on the right-hand side, follow the signposted entrance to The Worcestershire Way as it heads towards the corner of the Tank Quarry car park and through the very interesting Geological Trail. Thus, returning to the starting point of this short circular walk. Although the walk is just over two miles in total, the diversity of the scenery has made it a pleasurable couple of hours, enjoying the attractive North Malvern Hills.

Notes and observations from walk 1

alvern Link

History

The history of
the Link can
be traced back
some 3,000
years ago,
suggested by
the discovery
of a Bronze
Age axe head
in 1780. A
comparable
find in
Mathon,
excavated in
1905, links the
two similarly
fashioned

weapons with the first tribespeople who populated
the Malverns. Much later in 140-150 A.D., potters
left their mark on the Link countryside with the
remains of kilns, drying buildings and waste
tips of rejected bowls, jars, tankards, flagons and
other ceramic household items.

The Romans had departed England by 418 A.D, and then followed three hundred years of unrest with the Saxon invasion and wars between rival tribal kingdoms. With the settling influence of Christianity, Pershore Abbey was founded in 686A.D. By the ninth century, records show that the Abbey was given a large estate by a Saxon landowner named Beonorth. This formed the Saxon manor of Leigh. The manor charter describes the boundaries of the estate by defining two landmarks: the southern boundary, which is now the Worcester Road running through the Link and a ridge which is assumed to lie at the base of the Malvern Hills.

The boundary between the manors of Leigh and Powick was marked by a large stone, now called the Link Stone. The Link Stone is the oldest monument in the Link and is located in the churchyard of St Matthias near the Hampden Road entrance. It was used at one time to collect dues for the right of passage from travellers between the manors of Leigh and Powick.

The Link remained part of the manor of Leigh for several hundred years following the Norman Conquest in 1066. Part of the manor, however, had been given away by Edward the Confessor to support the finances for Westminster Abbey, and was known as the Link Walk. William the Conqueror then followed, who made a significant change to the Link after the death of his Queen Matilda in 1083, by converting the estate into a 'Chase'. The forested Chase had its King's Keeper, based in Hanley Castle which was then the administration centre for the area. The deer in the Chase were protected by a royal decree, thus providing a wealth of sport when royalty occasionally visited; their skins were tanned in the Link, in the area of Tanhouse Lane. The cleared areas at the time were farmed under the continuing local influence of Pershore Abbey. The inhabitants had to serve two masters, their landlords, the monks, and the King's Keeper.

After the dissolution of the monasteries between 1538 and 1540, the manor of Leigh passed from possession of Pershore Abbey to the Crown. In 1576, Queen Elizabeth 1 gave it to Christopher Hatton, her Master of the Horse. A few years later Hatton relinquished this title, and in 1590 the Queen made a fresh grant to Edmund Colles, Justice of the Shire. The Colles were natives of Leigh and had acted as stewards for Pershore

Abbey. Their memorial slabs can be seen in Leigh Church and date back to 1495. The Colles retained their status as 'Lords of the Manor' until 1615, when debt forced the sale of the

estate to Sir Walter Devereux, who was the sheriff for the County of Worcestershire and Member of Parliament. In 1628 King Charles 1 intended to raise money by deforesting the Chase and partially succeeded by selling the Link Walk. Local opposition from landowners prevented the sale of the rest of the Chase until the reign of his son, Charles II.

Sir Walter Devereux purchased the Link and reunited the Link with the manor of Leigh. The area gradually developed from forest to farmland and onto commercialisation. The manufacture of bricks was recorded from 1633 in the Lower Howsell Road area.

Sir Walter was succeeded by his second son Leicester Devereux; his eldest son tragically drowned when he attempted to cross the frozen River Teme in February 1658.

In 1742, following the deaths of the Devereux descendants, who were without heirs, the estate was purchased by James Cocks, who was Member of Parliament for Reigate in Surrey. It was inherited by his son James in 1750, who was killed whilst fighting in France in 1758. The heir was his uncle, the Reverend John Cocks. A more detailed account of the Cocks is described in walk 11, where the inscription of the fortunes of the Cocks family is described on the Obelisk.

John Cocks had been the Rector of Leigh since 1755. His son, Charles Cocks of Eastnor, was created Baron Somers of Evesham in 1784. After his death in 1806, his son, John Somers Cocks was created firstly Viscount Eastnor and secondly Earl Somers. The first Earl Somers died in 1841, and was followed by his second son, John Somers Cocks who died in 1852. John Somers provided the site for St. Matthias's Church (the current home of the Link Stone) and the family name has been adopted by the nearby Somers Park Primary School in Church Road. The third Earl Charles Somers sold most of their land in the Link to private owners and builders. The earldom became extinct in 1882. The present descendant of

the Somers-Cocks family is the Hon. Mrs Hervey-Bathurst, daughter of the late Lord Somers, who resides in Eastnor Castle.

The Birth of the British Motor Industry

During the late 1800's, British motoring history had its roots in Malvern Link. It is interesting to record that the first motor vehicle manufacturer in Malvern was Charles Santler, along with his brother Walter, who produced their first steam-powered vehicle in 1889. Some reports suggest that this was the first motor car manufactured in the United Kingdom. By the early 1920's they had brought out a three-wheeler car, marketed as the 'Rushabout', which was an imitation of the Morgan Runabout.

Harry Morgan, the founder of the Morgan Motor Company, moved to Malvern Link from Swindon in 1906, and established himself as a garage owner. His first vehicle, a single-seater, twin-cylinder prototype was built in 1909, and put into production the following year. The Runabout was exhibited at the very first motor show at Olympia in 1910.

In 1912, the Morgan Motor Company was formed with capital support from Harry Morgan's father. Harrods of Knightsbridge acted as agents for the Runabout. Over the next 15 years Harry Morgan developed the chassis and engine, and by 1925, the Morgan was the fastest three-wheeled vehicle in the world, and the rest, as they say is history!

The famous Morgan Motor Company is located some 400 metres from the Malvern Link crossroad in Pickersleigh Road. Map reference SO 7872 4730. To observe the manufacture (mainly by hand-crafted techniques) of these iconic vehicles, is by appointment only. Telephone the main reception on 01684 573104.

The recently opened Visitors Centre, a short distance from the front of the factory down Spring Lane, provides informative video presentations, a small museum and shop. For guided museum tours weekdays only, telephone 01684 584580. For more information, the website address is www.morgan-motor.co.uk.

view of North Hill and Worcestershire Beacon from Lower Hoswell Rod

Walk 2

 alvern Link to North Hill via Cowleigh. Returning by St Ann's Well and Great Malvern

Malvern Link looking towards North Hill

Summary.

A culturally interesting and diverse circular walk of 6.1 miles, which can be started at any point and provides shorter 'opting out' routes if the weather is inclement. The walk meanders through open farmland and cider apple orchards and takes in a section of the Worcestershire Way.

Following there is a fairly steep path, accessing the Lady Howard De Walden Drive as it circumnavigates North Hill.

There is an opportunity to reach the summit of North Hill (397 metres), and afterwards a pleasant downhill trot to St Ann's Well. After a refreshing drink of Malvern's finest spring water, take some time to visit the historic Great Malvern town centre and

View of End Hill from the Lower Howsell Playing fields

return via Elgar's House, the Link Common and the residential areas of Malvern Link.

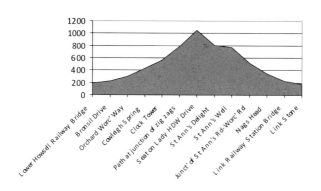

Distance, time and altitude.

6.1 miles. Allow a minimum of three hours without refreshment breaks or other stops for the complete tour. The summit of North Hill is 397 metres (1,303 feet).

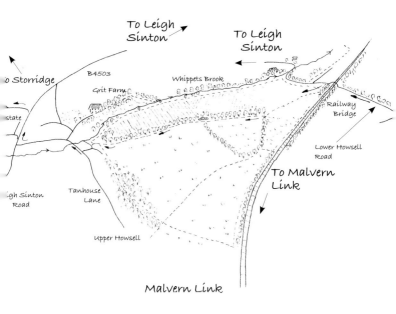

Refreshments

St Ann's Well

Bluebird
Tea Rooms

The New Inn

The Nag's Head

The Star Inn

Wells, Springs and Spouts

St Ann's Well

The Cowleigh Spout

The Temperance Drinking Fountain (now dry, no pun intended!).

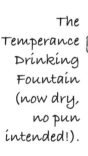

This little 'quip' is now out of date following the recent renovation of the fountain!

Malvhina Spring

Places and points of int

Mid
Nineteenth
Century
Pillar Box

The Clock Tower

The 'Link Stone'

'Forli'
Elgar's
House

Connections to other walks
Walk 3. Town Centre to St Ann's Well
Walk 14. All the Hills, End to End with the help of the 'Hopper' Bus
Walk 15. The Worcestershire Way

This circular walk can be joined at any point. However, because it is probably better to end the walk coming downhill, the walk commences at the lowest point in Lower Howsell Road at the railway bridge. This can be accessed from the junction of Worcester Road and Lower Howsell Road in Malvern Link map reference SO 7869 4897, or from Leigh Sinton at the junction of Leigh Sinton Road (B4503) and the Malvern Road.

Lower Howsell Road and the surrounding area was intensively used by the Romans for the pottery production of Malvernian and Severn Valley Ware. This was an important industry and produced much of the pottery used in the West Midlands and beyond. A kiln was excavated between Lower Howsell and Newland. There are a couple of medieval cottages, such as Cromwell Cottage dating back to circa 1390, and several seventeenth century timber-framed buildings provide a post-medieval historical backdrop to this mainly modern twentieth century developed area of Malvern Link.

For those arriving by train, the walk can begin
from Malvern Link Railway Station, which first
opened for business in much grander settings
in 1859. The only
remains of its

bygone era are the black-painted wrought iron
gates, hidden behind
the wooden waiting room on
Platform Two, which once
led to a large Gothic-styled
hotel. This was demolished
after much public outcry,
and sadly replaced by 1960's
flats and garages.

Leave the station from the Platform One entrance, by heading across the car park. Note the attractive lamps on the Malvern stone entrance pillars.

Turn left, heading north-east down the Worcester Road, past the fire station and cross-roads.

On the left is a recently built residential home. This is Santler Court; note the burgundy coloured plaque depicting the original location of the Morgan Motor Company. H.F.S Morgan opened a garage and motor works on this site. He ran a successful 15-seater motor bus service between the Link and Malvern Wells, and later between Malvern and Gloucester. He designed and built the three-wheeler 'Runabout' here, launching his career as a motor-vehicle manufacturer.

Continue into the Link. At the junction of the
second road on the left by the chemist's shop is a
small tiled water feature
known as the 'Link
Spring' (although
I have only seen
water flowing once
in nine years!).
Information about
this sculpture can
be seen on the wall
of the chemist shop.

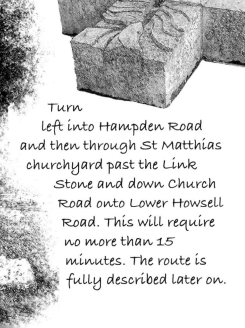

Turn
left into Hampden Road
and then through St Matthias
churchyard past the Link
Stone and down Church
Road onto Lower Howsell
Road. This will require
no more than 15
minutes. The route is
fully described later on.

If approaching from the Worcester Road turn

into Lower Howsell Road, continue past the playing fields on the left and the New Inn. If arriving by car, it is suggested that once past Church Road, park in the next available space, especially at weekends when visiting junior football teams reduce the traffic to a single file. The Howsells is the last small cul-de-sac before the railway bridge. It is very small and not suitable for additional vehicles.

Thus, having arrived or parked on Lower Howsell Road, head away from Malvern Link towards Leigh Sinton and the railway bridge.

The remains of a cast iron drinking fountain can be seen in the corner of the playing fields next to the attractive thatch roofed Summerfield Cottage.

Note that many of the older houses on the right such as the large Summerfield House, the 'black and white' Cromwell Cottage, have their 'backs' to the road. This is because Lower Howsell Road once took a different route further to the north. The current road was merely a track. During the development of the railway in 1859, the present road took prominence.

Elms Farm is the last dwelling on the right-hand side (looking east) before the railway bridge and is an impressive Georgian farmhouse.

For information, the signposted footpath next to Elms Farm ends up just a stone's throw from the popular Swan Inn on Stocks Lane in Newland, and can be reached after half a mile or so of easy walking across farm land.

Back to the route, the footpath can be easily missed; it is accessed on the Leigh Sinton side of the railway bridge, map reference SO 7868 4897 and turns left (due west), parallel, but a safe distance away from the railway line.

Emerging out of a small copse, a footpath continues alongside the railway line embankment. The walk follows the quite obviously well-trodden path across the centre of the field, towards a line of trees separating the two fields.

Here, looking south-west, the full splendour of the northern-most hills can be seen, dominated by North Hill.

The footpath follows the western (left-hand) side of the hedge and trees. At the junction of the next field is a small footbridge by a pond on the right. Continue, keeping the hedge to the right.

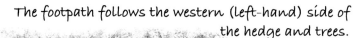

Here, sadly, are a number of oak trees which have been destroyed by ivy.

During springtime the number of rabbits to be seen along this path is considerable.

The path
terminates
at the metal
'kissing
gate', map
reference SO
7780 4871,
in Bronsil
Drive,
which will
cause problems
if cycling; however the
adjacent large farm gate may allow
a bike to be carried over. Thus far the distance
travelled is 0.6 miles.

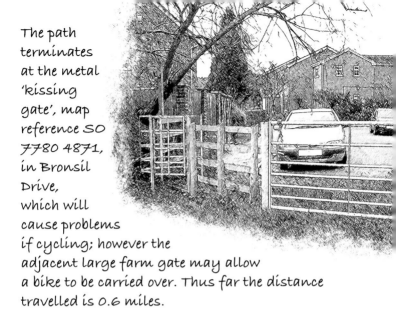

A short walk along Bronsil Drive past modern
houses, heading south-west for 50 metres or so,
leads into Tanhouse Lane. Turn right and look
carefully for Whippits Brook (which has its origin
in West Malvern) and follow the
lane that derives its name from
the local tanning industry,
which decimated the

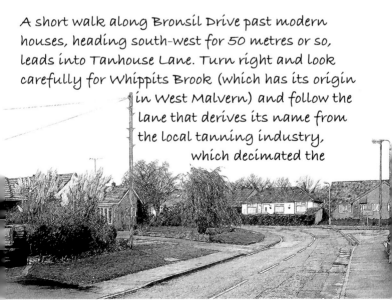

Chase deer during the Elizabethan era. Follow the road around a sweeping left-hand bend and continue for another two hundred metres to where the lane joins the Leigh Sinton Road.

Turn right here towards Leigh Sinton and after walking a short way, take a left, turning through the housing estate via Westwood Road and right into Halfkey Road. Or alternatively continue further along the Leigh Sinton Road for a few hundred metres and turn left into Halfkey Road. Fragments of pottery preceding the Romans have been found around this area.

Halfkey Road turns off right through fields towards Halfkey Farm and eventually the Hereford Road. However, keeping the houses to the left, the road is now signposted Hospital Road. Continue for a further 300 metres, passing several small Culs-de-sac on the left and on the right a number of Malverns famous gas lamps, which are still in working order.

The house on the corner of Redwing Close is in fact the old hospital for tuberculosis sufferers, indicated by the sign set into the brick wall, '1900 Malvern Hills District Council'.

Just after the last house and private road is the public footpath. This follows the course of a small brook and hedgerow. If it looks overgrown, the tractor path to the left of the stream provides access to the cider apple orchards beyond.

This tractor path during winter, can be quite churned up and muddy. For information, at the junction where the footpath meets the tractor path, there is a footpath heading across the fields in a northerly direction towards Crumpton Hill Road.

Keeping the hedge on the right, follow the tractor path skirting the edge of the orchard. In spring the glorious pink and white apple blossom is well worth seeing.

A few hundred metres further on there is a large track which crosses the centre of the orchard. This is where the junction of the Worcestershire Way and a second public footpath to Crumpton Hill Road meet, map reference SO 7679 4861. Our route is to turn left, moving through the centre of the orchard in the direction of North Hill, which is due west following the Worcestershire Way.

A pleasant extension to this walk, particularly at weekends, is to turn right in a north-westerly direction following either of the two footpaths

heading towards Crumpton Hill Road and north onto Storridge. Here, during the weekends only, Knights Cider is open to the public, providing an opportunity to sample some of Worcestershire's finest draught cider. Free tasting is encouraged and it is advisable that if arriving by car, the driver is forcibly limited in their volume of imbibing!

Back to our route, traversing the orchard, there is a
substantial wooden seat providing the weary with
fine views of the valley.

Enter the open fields through a new galvanised
kissing gate; to the right is
a small hill with delightful
grassy slopes, it
beckons to be run
up and then rolled
down, just for the
sheer fun of it.

Keeping to the footpath with the hedge to the left, Whippits Brook is reached after a short while, this time in the lee of several oak trees. This makes an excellent picnic spot where

children can play and make dams in the shallow spring water.

Crossing the bridge over Whippets Brook and being careful not to trip up on the cattle bars at ankle height, walk across the grassy knoll to the next stile.

the path leads uphill into a cider apple orchard of young trees. Alternatively take the footpath to the left, which shortens the walk and leads on to Cales Farm and back into North Malvern via Broadlands Drive and Cowleigh Bank.

Continuing our walk, enter the orchard over the stile; the Worcestershire Way skirts the woods to the left and climbs uphill. Nearing the end of the orchard, the path disappears into the corner of the woods through another galvanised gate and a short run of steps leads down onto a farm track. Keeping left here leads to a viewpoint facing directly towards End Hill and North Hill. Looking left, here is a glorious view of North Malvern, Malvern Link and over in the distance the Severn Valley and the Old Hills at Callow.

Following the wide farm track, head gently downhill towards the first of the Malvern Hills, called End Hill 1,079 ft (329m). There will probably be horses in the field to the right, who seem to appear to particularly enjoy human company with a gentle rub to their noses-please note the sign asking not to feed them!

Exiting the track through a gate to meet the Cowleigh Road (B4219), turning right would lead to Storridge (no footpaths, many blind bends, so not advisable for walking). So turn left past Cowleigh Park Farm, which was built in 1620, with a history dating back to the thirteenth century. Bed & Breakfast and holiday accommodation is available. It has Malvern spring water from the Cowleigh Spring on tap. Telephone number 01684 566750.

Just a few metres further on is the first Malvern spring on this walk, known locally as the Cowleigh Spring, but

officially titled the Earl of Beauchamp Fountain. This was built in 1905, replacing the original spout. Map reference SO 7664 4753. Thus far the distance is 1.9 miles.

The flow rate from the spring is quite substantial and it is likely to get one's feet wet whilst enjoying the pure elixir of the Malvern Hills. This spring is famous for its supply of fresh spring water, even in times of drought.

Tucked behind the spring is a small
car park with an information
board describing the
installation and use
of the spring over
the centuries.

The tanks behind
the spring used
to feed the
Madresfield
Court Estate
some three
miles away.
The tanks
still
continue
to supply
Cowleigh
Park Farm.
Apparently
the Earl of
Madresfield
linked up the
farm in 1919, to provide the
tenants with free water as
a reward for their services to the armed forces
during the First World War.

For information, the Worcestershire Way continues up the hill behind and to the left of the spring, initially up a flight of steps and across an open field to the Old Hollow Road. However, continue east along the Cowleigh Road for a few hundred metres into North Malvern.

The very pleasant Star Inn is just a short distance further on, past a cider mill set outside an antiques shop. This is a fine gastro pub which

provides excellent Cantonese cuisine and boasts CAMRA approved real ales, telephone 01684 891918.

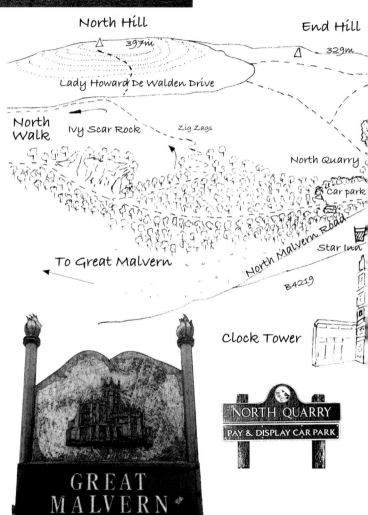

North Hill

△ 397m

End Hill

△ 329m

Lady Howard De Walden Drive

North Walk

Ivy Scar Rock

Zig Zags

North Quarry

Car park

To Great Malvern

North Malvern Road

Star Inn

B4219

Clock Tower

GREAT MALVERN

NORTH QUARRY
PAY & DISPLAY CAR PARK

Worcestershire
WEST MALVERN
Please drive carefully

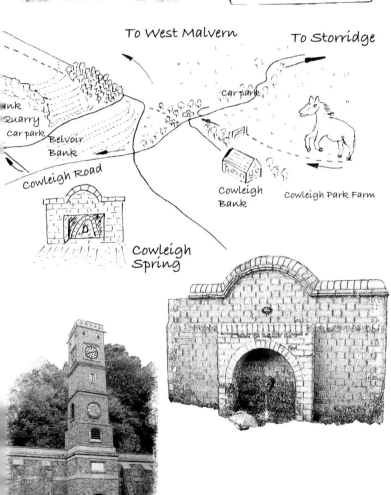

To West Malvern

To Storridge

Car park

nk
Quarry
Car park

Belvoir
Bank

Cowleigh Road

Cowleigh
Bank

Cowleigh Park Farm

Cowleigh
Spring

However, if choosing to ignore a pint of Wyre Piddle and crispy aromatic duck,

take a right turn up the steep road of Belvoir Bank. At the top is the large three-storey North Hill House, which before conversion to flats was a hostelry. Belvoir Bank heads up to the junction with the North Malvern Road, and turning left (south-west) the refurbished clock tower can be seen (map reference SO 7698 4706).

This was built in 1843, and paid for by Charles Morris (1799-1856), who was a major benefactor for North Malvern. He was the grandson of James Morris, Deputy Lieutenant of Surrey and High Sheriff. The Clock Tower was built for the benefit of the local inhabitants.

Originally the circular inscription, dated 1901, was the location for the clock face. However, in 1901 the Urban District Council took on the repairs and extended the height of the tower with the permission of the owner, Mr C W Dyson Perrins (of Lee and Perrins Worcestershire Sauce fame).

After 106 years the Clock Tower was subject to a timely refurbishment during 2007, this time with money made available through the National Heritage Lottery Fund. The Clock Tower was in quite a poor state and was in danger of being irrevocably damaged by the growth of nearby trees. These were cut down, the brickwork repointed, the clock repaired, and a new set of attractive wrought iron gates now proudly protect the interior.

Continue a short distance down the road (south-east) towards Great Malvern and into the very large North Hill Quarry car park, run by the Conservators. On entering the  large car park keep left; the metalled track starts to climb past a couple of houses nestling in the side of the hill.

Further along, the path splits into two; stay with the higher path to the right. The view here is obscured in the summer due to the foliage of the young

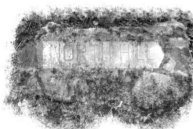

deciduous trees. On reaching a sign for North Hill, which is located on the hillside at ankle height on the right, head towards North Hill map reference SO 7732 4638; take the smaller path heading north which is quite steep in places. It zigzags north-south up North Hill through bright yellow gorse in spring and strikingly purple foxgloves in summer to provide a glorious view over Great Malvern.

Continue to climb the steep narrow path; as the trees and gorse are left behind the open expanse of the hills becomes apparent. Shortly after, join a wide path named 'Lady Howard De Walden Drive'. The path or 'Drive' carves a large, horizontal scar into the hillside, which is visible many miles away.

A fascinating story lies behind Lady Howard De Walden, who had this path constructed for her use; it was claimed she owned more houses than anyone else in the world. She died in 1899, and furthermore, her obituary described her as the most eccentric woman in Britain!

At this point in our walk, turn left (due west) heading for the Beacon which is the highest point looking left (south) at 1,395 feet (425m). However, there is also an option to enjoy a steep scramble to reach the summit of North Hill. Turn right, and just a short distance further on there is a path heading up the steep hillside.

view of Beacon from 'The Saddle' between End Hill and North Hill

The path, if viewed from a distance, creates a near vertical scar on the hillside.

photograph courtesy of Sabine Gupta

On approaching the summit the slope is less demanding and provides a very worthwhile panorama of the counties of Worcestershire and Herefordshire.

view from North Hill and vertical path

After enjoying the view, either retrace one's steps to the 'Drive' or head west and follow the largest of the paths down towards the nape of the valley where there is a conveniently located seat. A short distance further on, there is a path heading down through Green Valley.

view from North Hill looking towards End Hill

If not partaking of the scramble to the summit
of North Hill, continue to follow the broad 'Lady
Howard De Walden Drive'. There are a number of
seats strategically placed to rest and picnic upon.
The walk here is more or less flat and is popular
during the weekends with locals and tourists
alike. The 'Drive' dominates the route around
North Hill and below is the attractive Green
Valley. As the Drive meets the top of the valley
a little height is lost and joins the junction of a
number of paths, map reference SO 7672 4598.

To continue straight on here, will, as the sign describes, lead to the 'Saddle', the point between Sugarloaf Hill 1,207ft (368m) and the Beacon 1,395 ft (425m). This section of the walk now joins the Beacon Race Walk as described in Book 2.

The walk heads down the upper section of Green Valley, now quite thickly wooded with predominantly sycamore trees. However, at the turn of the twentieth century, this valley was bare of trees and not as attractive as it is now.

The path down the valley is fairly steep in places and after rain can expose the edges of large stones, just waiting to trip up the unwary! To the right, the bank rises sharply, and to the left the bank drops away again quite steeply into the depths of the valley. Continue downhill until arriving at a junction, and take the right fork to St Ann's Well. However, before doing so, just a few metres straight on from the junction there is a grassy plateau

known as St Ann's delight, map reference SO 7719 4585; here is a seat, picnic area and fine views of Malvern.

Turning left leads down into Green Valley along a substantial path featuring a planted avenue of

sycamore trees; this broadens into the Happy Valley Road, which descends steeply into Great Malvern at the junction of the Worcester Road. Returning to the walk and looking

to the right (south), is St Ann's Well, map reference SO 7723 4580. This is where one can enjoy a well-earned rest / watering stop after covering 3.7 miles of the walk. Possibly sampling some freshly cooked vegetarian food. Toilets are available just below the café near the pond

(see Book 2, where a more in-depth study of

St Ann's Well is described). Inside the building above the sculptured well basin and spout is an inscription recounting that St Ann was the mother of Mary, the mother of Jesus. The inscription goes on to illustrate that blind George Pullin played his harmonium outside St Ann's. In 1892, Lady Foley honoured 'blind George' with the tablet inset into the wall.

IN MEMORY OF GEORGE PULLEN, "BLIND GEORGE" WHO FOR OVER 50 YEARS PLAYED HIS HARMONIUM AT ST ANN'S WELL, DIED FEB. 23RD 1936.

Walking down the somewhat narrow and steep path to St Ann's Well, judge for yourself whether Tolkien gained inspiration and imagined the small rounded building nestling amongst the trees and hillside as a burrow for his hobbits! The café is eclectic in its fare and opening times (typically only weekends and Bank holidays from 10 am to 4 pm during the colder months); however the entrance to the spring is open most of the time and provides a refreshing drink of Malverns finest.

The short downhill walk to Great Malvern is on a metalled surface and is very steep, and care must be taken when it is frosty or wet.

The Worcestershire Way signpost clearly identifies the route. However, at the junction of the path and the sign marked 'Halfway', take a right here, and keeping to the left of the road, tucked in the

corner is the public footpath which descends for some 97 steps (rather than the stated 99) to Rosebank Gardens.

Maybe count them for yourself and make up your own mind? A seat is provided part way, presumably for those walking up, to rest, rather than for those walking down.

The gardens are quite pleasant and home to a large population of rabbits. Rosebank Gardens is the starting point for the annual Beacon Race (see Book 2).

The plaque in the garden is in memory of Sir Edward Elgar, 1857-1934. There are roses planted to commemorate the 150th anniversary of his birth.

The information board on the brick wall separating the gardens from the Mount Pleasant Hotel provides details of the house which was formerly built here. Dyson Perrins, who owned the grounds to the demolished house, developed the gardens for the enjoyment of the general public in 1918 into what can be seen today.

Walking down the path beside the wall to the Mount Pleasant Hotel, the Wells Road is reached.

Here on the right is an attractive Victorian bus stop to keep one dry during inclement weather. Local buses to Barnards Green and Ledbury (Route Number 675 & 363) and National Express coaches to London stop here, and it is designated as bus stop 'E,' Rosebank Gardens.

Taking a left here towards the famous Victorian developed Belle Vue Terrace and crossing the road into the terraced grounds, the route leads to the Malvhina Fountain in all her glory.

Malvhina

This is the central and most accessible spring in Great Malvern and is the start and finish point of the Worcestershire Way (see book 4).

Looking across Church
Street from the
Malvhina Fountain
and few metres further
on past two old piano's
adorned with flowers
and Elgar's statue
are Malverns premier
purveyor of beverages
and light lunches, the
Bluebird Tea Rooms.

Church Street is a
busy thoroughfare and
incredibly steep outside the
tearooms and the junction
to the Worcester Road. It is quite fun watching
how drivers cope with the steep hill climb and
pull away against the busy traffic flow on the
Worcester
Road.

'Forli'
Elgar's House

Link Top

To Malvern Link

Zig Zags

The Nags
Head Pub

Link Common

car park

North Hill
397m Δ

North
Malvern
Road

Cockshot Road

Lady Howard
De Waldron
Drive

North
Walk

Graham
Road

Montreal House

Green valley

Red Lion
Pub

The Bluebird
Tea Rooms

Happy
valley

St Ann;s
Road

Belle
Vue
Terrace

Church Street

Great Malvern

St Ann's Well

The Priory Gutehouse
Malvern Museum of
Local History

Heading out
of Belle Vue
Island walk
down the steps
opposite the
Post Office,
then turn
left,
cross the
road and
continue
uphill past
the Bluebird
Tea Rooms
and the
HSBC
Bank,
which
during
Edwardian
times was
a cake
shop!
Straight
ahead is
Barclays
Bank,
housed in an
impressive building, which was the Royal Library
in the 1900's.

127

On the opposite side is 'The Unicorn', which is reputed to be Malvern's oldest public house. It is said that C.S. Lewis enjoyed a pint or two of the local brew here, and after one of his sojourns to

this hostelry one evening, he noticed the inviting glow of the gas lamp on the main road, which gave him the inspiration for the entrance to Narnia.

Continue past the Nationwide Building Society and the adjoining Whately Recordon Solicitors, which was the previous site of the famous water cure, Coburg Bath House. This was fed from the Green Valley spring water and featured in its heyday both hot and cold spring baths. It was built in 1822, and was

in use up to 1852. The Foley Arms Hotel is a short distance further along the Worcester Road, followed by seven splendid Regency period houses, both Sydney House and Breedon House offer bed and breakfast. Further along at Number 44, opposite the carpet and interiors shop, is Montreal House. This is where Charles Darwin made his second visit to Malvern for the water cure for his

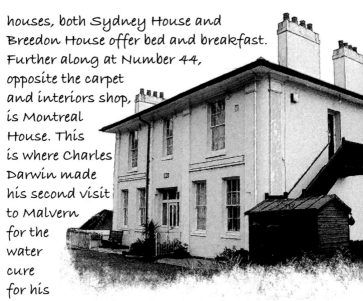

daughter and himself under the supervision of Dr James Gully, and where sadly his daughter Anne died.

The blue plaque was unveiled by his great-great-grandson Randal Keynes in 2009 to commemorate the bicentenary of the birth of Darwin. Anne is buried in Malvern Priory.

MHDC

In 1851 CHARLES DARWIN stayed here with his daughter ANNE ELIZABETH who was being treated by pioneer of the Malvern Water Cure DR JAMES MANBY GULLY

MALVERN CIVIC SOCIETY

A few hundred metres further on take a right turn down Bank Street, which is quite a steep downhill path. It crosses Zetland Road and ends up at the junction to one of Malverns finest watering holes, the Nag's Head on the corner of Moorlands Road and Lyggon Bank. This was voted CAMRA's top pub in 2007. Map reference SO 7767 4689. Telephone 01684 574373.

The Nag's Head from Link Common

Continue downhill along Moorlands Road from
the Nag's Head, to the junction of Graham Road.
There are a choice of routes; either turn left along
Graham Road and then turn right onto the
Worcester Road,
or continue straight
on from
the
cross-
roads
and
take a
left
at Cockshot Road
to the Worcester Road. Or be entirely reckless
and walk across the Link Common towards the
railway bridge, near Malvern Link station.

There is, however, an opportunity to ignore the various options described and make a slight deviation to see the house named 'Forli' in Alexandra Road. This is where Elgar lived between  1889 and 1898. He wrote the Enigma Variations and Imperial March whilst living here.

If so inclined to visit Forli, head uphill along Moorlands Road, and then, taking care at this busy corner of the Worcester Road known as Link Top, cross over by the general stores and head downhill for a very short way. On the left is Alexandra Road. Many of the houses here date back to the 1700's, and are quite impressive.

Number 37 is on the left hand side after approximately 300 metres and can be easily missed, as it is set back from the road along a substantial driveway. The only evidence of this historic place is a small plaque on the pillar of the garden wall. Retrace one's steps back to the Worcester Road and then enjoy the gentle downhill perambulation towards Malvern Link.

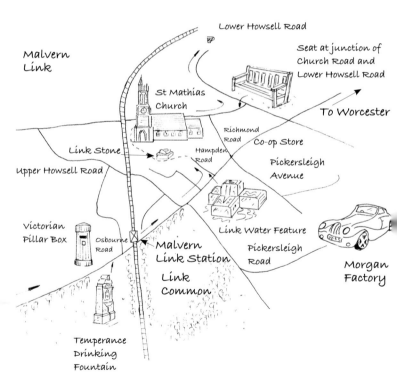

Approximately 100 metres west from the railway line and Malvern Link Station is the aptly named, now dry, Temperance Drinking Fountain

(note, recent repairs have returned it to its rightful purpose)

map reference SO 7818 4738. This elaborate stone fountain was built in 1900.

Whosoever will let him take of the water of life freely

The other interesting Victorian artefact located near here, on the opposite side of the Worcester Road, is the red painted cast-iron postbox. It is one of only three surviving cast-iron pillar boxes in Malvern. The fluted design of a Greek pillar was made by Smith and Hawkes in 1857, and was designed by the Post Office in conjunction with the Government Department of Science and Art.

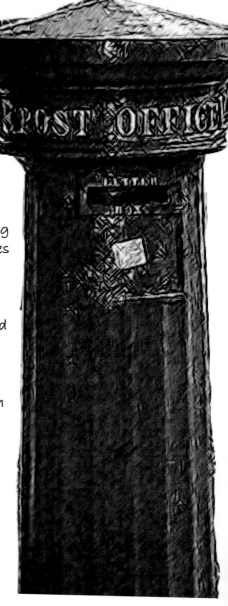

Head down the Worcester Road (north-east), past the new hospital and then cross the railway bridge by the Link Station, map reference SO 7820 4741. Go past the fire station and public toilets and over the cross-roads and continue downhill into the busy Malvern Link area. On the left is a recently built residential home. This is Santler Court; note the burgundy coloured plaque depicting the original location of the Morgan

fire station

Motor Company. H.F.S Morgan opened a garage and motor work on this site.

At the junction of the second road on the left by the chemist's shop is a small tiled water feature, there is information about the sculpture on the wall of the chemist  shop. Turning left into Hampden Road, walk a short distance to the footpath, which enters the graveyard of St Matthias Church.

Here is the Link Stone, which is the oldest monument in the Link. It was used at one time to collect dues for the right of passage between the manors of Leigh and Powick. It was moved from the junction of Pickersleigh Road with the Worcester Road to St Matthias Church some time after 1744.

Exiting the churchyard from the main entrance onto Church Road, turn right and continue to the junction of Lower Howsell Road. At the junction is a seat dedicated to Norman Caswell Sayer, who was killed during the First World War on Vimy Ridge during the battle of the Somme on April 10th 1917. He was a private, aged 28, serving with the City of Winnipeg Regiment. It is interesting to reflect that this walk encompasses history from the Romans through to the twentieth Century Turning left onto Lower Howsell Road will now conclude this thoroughly interesting circular walk.

Notes and observations from walk 2

Hostelries close to walks one and two

Please note that none of the establishments mentioned in this section provided food or beverages with the knowledge that I was collecting information for this guide. The opinions expressed are purely my own.

Great Malvern

St Ann's Well Cafe. A ten-minute hike up from Great Malvern, located in a fairytale setting. During the Victorian era, kidneys were roasted here for the hungry folk who were undergoing strict dieting along with the water cure. Nowadays its offering is vegetarian and is probably Malverns most popular source of free spring water. Telephone 01684 560285.

The Mount Pleasant Hotel next to the Rosebank Gardens offers accommodation, off-licence, restaurant and bars. Telephone 01684 561 837.

The Belle Vue Delicatessen, café and wine bar is located in the attractive Victorian Arcade in Belle Vue Terrace. It has a delightful curved window frontage and free Internet access. Telephone 01684 899333

The Ask Restaurant chain has recently opened up on Belle Vue Terrace. Do not forget to download your discount vouchers beforehand! Telephone 01684 893 500.

The Bluebird Tea Rooms (telephone 01684 561 166), located at number 9 Church Street, claims to have been Elgar's favourite tearooms and was established in 1913. During busy periods it is important to book in advance. The tea rooms which overlook the Elgar Statue and the Malvhina Spring are accessed by

stairs, the entrance is located on a particularly steep section of Church Street making access for the mobility-impaired nigh impossible.

The Unicorn, reputed to be Malverns oldest Inn. Number 2 Belle Vue Terrace. Telephone 01684 574152.

The Red Lion (St Ann's Well Road) Telephone 01684 564787, has good food and real ale at reasonable prices and probably represents the best food and beer combination in this part of Great Malvern.

Bengal Brasserie, Indian Restaurant. Telephone 01684 575091.

Hung's Kitchen, Chinese and English Cuisine. Telephone 01684 563063.

Foley Arms Hotel run by J D Weatherspoon.

The Nag's Head is probably Malverns premier real ale pub, with up to 16 cask ales on tap. It is located in the area known as 'Link Top' at the junction of Moorlands Road and Lygon Bank, which is a good 10 minutes walk from the centre of Great Malvern.

It has a heated terrace and a good quality restaurant. (Telephone 01684 574373).

Malvern Link

A good range of Indian restaurants can be found in Malvern Link. Paprika at Number 243 Worcester Road (Telephone 01684 569 820) in the centre of the Link's shops has been consistently regarded as 'good' in this neck of the Hills. Opposite in Fir Tree Walk (set back from the main road, with parking to the rear; watch out for wheel clampers if parking for other purposes) is Spice Cottage. It offers friendly service and because you can bring your own alcoholic drinks provides a good value night out. Telephone 01684 891217. Opposite is Premier Pizza which provides an alternative to the franchise mentioned overleaf.

Back on the Worcester Road a few metres away is May Link, Number 132 Worcester Road, (Telephone 01684 574940) the only Chinese restaurant and take away in this part of the Link. Domino's Pizza, Number 124 Worcester Road, (Telephone 01684 577 788) is close by.

Heading north out of Malvern Link on the Worcester Road opposite the Co-op is Vasai curry house. Although the name appears to change more frequently than we have leap years, it has always provided decent cuisine.
Telephone 01684 564400.

Lower Howsell Road has just the one pub along its twisting two-mile length, the New Inn. Telephone 01886 832359. It has a restaurant, a large beer garden, a play area for children and a spacious car park which might appeal to those embarking on walk two!

North Malvern
The very pleasant Star
Inn on the Cowleigh Road.
This is a fine gastro pub
which provides excellent
Cantonese cuisine and
boasts CAMRA approved
real ales, Telephone 01684
891918.

West Malvern
The Lamb Inn. Telephone
01684 577847. A very
popular pub with the
locals, and well worth a
visit.

Storridge
Knights Cider.
Crumpton Oaks, WR13
5HP. Telephone 01684
568887. Although
strictly not en-route,
this detour from
walk two was one of
those 'defining' moments after moving to
Malvern, which has remained with me as a
pleasantly tipsy memory. Here, during the
weekends Knights Cider is open to the public
and provides an opportunity to sample some of
Worcestershire's finest draught cider.

Bibliography

A big thanks to the helpful librarians in Malvern Library.

Bethell, Hal. Alarums and Excursions. A History of the Beacons and Bonfires on The Malvern Hills. First Paige, Malvern 1988.

Drake, Daphne. The Story of Malvern Link Worcestershire. First Paige, Malvern 1989.

Garrard, Rose. Malvern 'Hill of Fountains'.publications@garrardart.co.uk, 2006

Hastings, G. W. The Story of The Malverns. Cornish Brothers Ltd, 1911

Hurle, Pamela. Beneath the Malvern Hills. Russell Printers, 1973.

Hurle, Pamela. The Malverns. Phillimore, 1992.

Iles, Brian. Images of England. The Malverns. Tempus, 2005.

Laban, Brian. Morgan. First and Last of the Real Sports Cars. Virgin Books, 2000.

Smith, Brian S. A History of Malvern. Alan Sutton & The Malvern Bookshop 1978.

Waite, Vincent. Malvern Country. Phillimore 1979.

Weaver, Cora & Osborne, Bruce. Aquae Malvernensis. Aldine Press, 1994.

Woodcock, Roy. Walks Around the Malverns. Meridian Books, 2005.

Worcestershire County Council. Malvern. Walking and Cycling Map

Contributers

The following 'stars' have given freely their own time to check out and contribute to this book. Thanks guys!

Mike Bolton
Cyril Edwards
Joshua Flint
Natasha Flint
Robert Flint
Sylvia Flint
Jerry and Julia Greer
Sabine Gupta
Wendy Lewin
John Lucas
Nuala and Geoff Roberts
Su Savage
Geralt Williams

Equipment used to create this Guide

Garmin Etrex hand held GPS
Olympus WS-300M voice recorder
Olympus C-310 digital camera
Asus Eee PC 900
Samsung P28 laptop
Akvis software

Further information and useful resources, to help plan your visit to the Malvern Hills.

www.malvernwalks.co.uk This provides a link to the webpage, providing information about this book and others in this series. There is also an opportunity to write your comments, updates and corrections to the walks. Any feedback from readers is welcomed.

For further information about the Conservators log on to their website at www.malvernhills.org.uk

The Morgan Motor Company in Pickersleigh Road, Malvern Link has its website at www.morgan-motor.co.uk

Malverns local brewery
www.malvernhillsbrewery.co.uk

The following is a great resource for providing information about the springs and spouts located around the Hills.
http://www.thespasdirectory.com/discover_the_spa_research_fell.asp?i=35

A useful website describing aspects of concern and actions about this area of outstanding natural beauty
www.malvernhillsaonb.org.uk

The County Council website provides a wide range of information www.malvernhills.gov.uk

This website provides a number of walks described by local enthusiasts in the Malverns and further afield.
www.countrywalkers.co.uk

John Howes has dedicated a great deal of time and effort to provide a really comprehensive walking and cycling information site about the Malverns;
http://www.malverntrail.co.uk/walkingmalvern.htm

INDEX

A

Akvis 24

Alexandra Road 133

Aquae Malvernensis 22

Ask Restaurant 143

B

Bank Street 131

Baron Somers of Evesham 73

Barnards Green 123

Beacon Books 22

Beacon Race & Walk 53, 116, 122

Beacon-Worcestershire 77, 113

Belle Vue Delicatessen 143

Belle Vue Terrace & Island 22, 23, 122

Belvoir Bank 106, 108

Bengal Brasserie 144

Beonorth 69

Birmingham 17

Black Pear Bitter 65

Bluebird Tea Rooms 82, 125, 126, 145

Bredon Hills 20

Bredon House 130

British Camp 14, 20, 21

Broadlands Drive 101

Bronsil Drive 93

C

Cales Farm 101

CAMRA 131

Castlemorton Common 20

Charles I, II 71

Chase End 21

Church Road 73, 87, 88

Church Street 23, 125, 127

Clock Tower 25, 26, 29, 33, 36, 40, 43, 48, 83, 108

Coburg Bath House 129

Cocks James & Charles 72, 73

Cocks Reverend John 73

Cockshot Road 132

Colles Edmund 70, 71

Colwall 17

Conservators 11, 30, 31, 39

Co-op (Malvern Link) 149

Cowleigh 38

Cowleigh Bank 101

Cowleigh Park Farm 102, 104

Cowleigh Road 102

Cowleigh Spring
(see Earl of Beauchamp Fountain)

Cromwell Cottage 89

Crumpton Hill Road 96, 97, 98

D

Danzell Spring 35, 61

Darwin Charles &
Anne 130

Davereux Sir Walter
and Leicester 71, 72

De Waldren see Lady
Howard De Walden

Doctor Who 42

Domino's Pizza 146

Dyson Perrins 43, 109,
122

E

Eastnor and
Eastnor Castle 16, 20, 73

Earl of Beauchamp
Fountain 82, 103,

Edward the Confessor 70

Elgar Edward 12, 78,
122, 125,
133, 143

Elizabeth I 70

Elizabeth II 12

Elms Farm 90

End Hill 26, 33, 50,
102, 115

F

Fiennes Celia 6

Fire Station 86, 137

Foley Arms Hotel 129, 144

Forli (Elgar's House) 83, 133

Fromes Hill 14

G

Gardiner Quarry 30

Geological Trail 41, 66

Gloucester 16, 86

Graham Road 132

Great (Gt) Malvern 12, 14, 17,
20, 22, 25,
38, 62, 77,
78, 110,
111, 118,
120, 124,
142, 143,
144, 145

Great Malvern
Railway Station 20

Great Malvern
Delicatessen 22

Green Valley 51, 114,
115, 116,
118, 129

Gully James Dr 130

H.

Halfkey Road 94

Hampden Road 69, 87,
134, 138

Hanley Castle	70
Hanley Swan	20
Happy Valley	118
Harmony House	59
Harrods	75
Harvey Map	21
Hatton Christopher	70
Hereford	17
Herefordshire	35, 53
Hereford Road	94
Hervey-Bathurst	73
Hills Hopper Bus	18, 19, 20, 83
Hobbit	120
Hockilwah Villas	64
Hollybush	16, 20
Holy Trinity Church	39
Hospital Road	94
House of Lords	30, 31

J

Joyners Meadow	54

K

Kendalls Common	39
Keynes Randal	130
Knights Cider	18, 98, 147

L

Lady Foley	121
Lady Howard De Walden	36, 49, 50, 59, 78, 112, 115
Lamb Bank Road	62, 63
Lamb Inn	34, 147
Lechmere R	22
Ledbury	14, 16, 19, 20, 62, 123
Lee & Perrins	43, 10, 109
Leigh Church	71, 73
Leigh Sinton and Manor of Leigh	72, 73, 84, 89, 91, 94, 139
Leigh Sinton Road	94
Lewis C S	128
Link Common	78, 132
Link Spring	87
Link Stone	69, 73, 83, 87, 139
Link Top	19, 20, 133
Link Walk	70, 71
Little Malvern Priory	15
Lyttleton House Gallery	22
Lodge Drive	39
London Paddington, Victoria	17, 18

Lower Howsell Road 72, 83, 84, 86, 87, 88, 89, 140, 146

Lyggon Bank 131

M

Madresfield Court 104

Malvern Bookshop 22

Malvern Hills Act 30, 31

Malvern Hills Brewery 29, 37, 64, 65

Malvern Hills Conservators see Conservators

Malvern Hills District Council 95

Malvern Hills Outdoor Centre 41, 63

Malvern Link 17, 19, 20, 38, 50, 68, 74, 75, 77, 78, 84, 85, 89, 101, 132, 134, 135, 137, 145, 146, 147, 150, 153

Malvern Link Railway Station 17, 85, 132, 135,

Malvern Road 84

Malvern Priory Church 130

Malvern Wells 20, 86

Malvernian Tours 18, 19

Malvhina Spring 82, 124, 125, 143

Map Shop (Upton upon Severn) 23

May Link 147

Moorlands Road 131, 132, 133, 145

Morgan Harry 74, 86, 137

Morgan Motor Company 12, 74, 75, 76, 137, 150

Mathon 59, 68

Matilda (Queen) 70

Moel Bryn Bitter 65

Montreal House 130

Morris Charles & James & School 25, 43, 44, 45, 46, 108

Mount Pleasant Hotel 122, 123, 142

N

Nag's Head 81, 131, 132, 145

Narnia 12, 128

National Heritage Lottery Fund 43, 56, 109

Newland 85, 90

Newtown Road	18, 19	Pullin 'Blind George'	119
New Inn	81, 88, 146	Pickersleigh Road	75, 139, 150
Ninetynine steps	123		
Norman Conquesl	22, 70	Pre-Cambrian stone	29
North Hill	26, 29, 50, 51, 77, 78, 91, 108, 110, 111, 113, 114, 115	Premier Pizza	145, 146
		Price Quarry	30
		Post Office	127, 136
		Powick	69, 139
		Pyx, pixies, pig path	26
North Hill House	108		
North Malvern	21, 25, 29, 33, 38, 44, 46, 48, 66, 101, 105		
		Q	
		Quarry-see Gardiner, Price, North and Summer	
North Malvern Quarry & car park	29, 33, 38, 40, 45, 110		
		R	
North Malvern Road	33, 38, 39, 40, 42, 108	Red Lion Inn	144
		Redmarley D'Abitot	16
O		Redwing Close	95
Obelisk	72	Richmond Road	19
Old Hills	101	River Avon	20
Old Hollow Road	27, 63	River Severn	50, 52
Ordnance Survey Explorer Maps	20	River Teme	72, 74
Osborne Bruce	22, 148	Roget Peter & Catherine	28, 37, 58
		Romans	69, 84, 94, 140
P		Rosebank Gardens	121, 122, 123
Pershore Abbey	69, 70		
Pillar Box 19th Century	83, 136	Royal Library	127
		Runabout	74, 75, 86
Priory Steps	22	Rushabout	74

S

Santler Charles & Walter — 74

Santler Court — 86, 137

Saxon — 69

Sayer Norman Caswell — 140

Severn Valley Ware — 84

Shropshire — 6, 33, 51

Smith & Hawkes — 136

Smith Brian — 22, 148

Somers-Cocks, John — 73

Somers Park Primary School — 73, 75

Somme — 140

Spice Cottage — 145

Spring Lane — 76

Star Inn, North Malvern — 81, 105, 147

St Aldwyn — 26

St Ann's Delight — 117

St Anns Well & Cafe — 38, 77, 78, 80, 84, 82, 117, 118, 119, 120, 142

St James's Church — 28, 37, 53

St James's School — 37, 53, 56, 57, 59

St Matthias Church, Malvern Link — 69, 73, 87, 138, 139

St Werstan — 26

Stocks & Whipping Post — 35, 38

Stocks Lane — 90

Storridge — 14, 98, 102, 147

Sugarloaf Hill — 116

Summer Quarry — 30

Summerfield House & Cottage — 89

Swan Inn, Newland — 90

T

Table Hill — 33, 34, 50, 51, 53

Tanhouse Lane — 70, 93

Tank Quarry & car park — 33, 38, 41, 42, 50, 66

Temperance Drinking Fountain — 82, 135

Tewkesbury — 13

Thesaurus of English Words and Phrases see Roget

Three Counties Showground — 13, 14, 20

Tourist Information Centre (TIC) — 23

Tolkien JRR — 12, 120

Tuberculosis — 95

U

Unicorn Inn — 128, 144